MW00834967

Levinson's book-length poem, *The Sauntering*, is a hypnotic journey on a literal and metaphorical walking trail. The narrator draws on spiritual tradition, familial loss, and a life of books to form meaning from the act of walking itself. With visceral rhythms, Levinson transcends the personal and connects his reader to the geography of an expanded world—a poet who, if he had the means, would "walk the world entire."

—Jessica Cuello, author of *Liar* and *Yours, Creature*

Poet Zev Levinson's second book, *The Sauntering*, is aptly named. Levinson's autobiographical, book-length poem embodies the act of walking, permeated with a quiet stillness and with the consistent rhythm of quatrains that journey us through boyhood, the tragic death of a parent, and even love. This meditative tale offers us a sense of one poet's growth through the transformative principles of forward motion, the presence of ritualistic faith, and a deep connection to the natural world. It is a true adventure to be able to go on this trip of many trips with Levinson. How many are given a chance to touch the Sphinx in Egypt, then almost be killed by a fall from a very different stone in the space of a few pages? Levinson says, "The walking is the breath of all" and we are brought alive with each breath as we engage with the vivid lines and unquestionable spiritual and emotional sustenance of this book.

—Jennifer Militello, author of *The Pact*

THE
SAUNTERING

ZEV LEVINSON

ILLUSTRATED BY STACY BECKER

The Sauntering

Text Copyright © 2024 by Zev Levinson

Illustrations copyright by Stacy Becker © 2023. All rights reserved. The pdf
e-version of this work is licensed to Cal Poly Humboldt Press under a Creative
Commons Attribution-NonCommercial-NoDerivatives 4.0 International License.

Beyond the above, no part of this publication may be reproduced, stored in or
introduced into a retrieval system, or transmitted, in any form, or by any means,
electronic, mechanical, photocopying, recording, or otherwise, without the prior written
permission of the copyright owner. To request permission, please contact the publisher.

Published by SequoiaSong Publications
PO Box 2551
McKinleyville, CA 95519
info@sequoiasong.com

Digital PDF Creative Commons Publisher
Cal Poly Humboldt Press
1 Harpst Street
Arcata, CA 95521-8299

Publisher's Cataloging-in-Publication Data
Names: Levinson, Zev, 1966-
Title: The Sauntering / by Zev Levinson.
Description: First trade paperback original edition. / Arcata [California]:
SequoiaSong Publications, 2024. / Includes illustrations by Stacy Becker.
Identifiers: LCCN 2024931559 / ISBN-13: 979-8-9865440-2-1 (pbk.)
Subjects: Poetry—21st century. / Prose poems, American. / Humboldt County
(Calif.)—Poetry. / Travel—Poetry.

Interior design, layout and editing by CM Phillips
Cover Design by CM Phillips
Set in Adobe Garamond type

*For my mother Fay and my fathers Joe Vela
and Robert Levinson. You are still setting the
pace, sometimes at the speed of dachshunds,
sometimes elephant seals.*

How much
do you need to walk
until,
like everyone,
instead of walking on the surface,
we rest under the earth?

       *

...I proclaim you
path
and not shroud,
pristine
staircase
with steps
of air . . .
~Pablo Neruda, "Ode to Age," translated by Ilan Stavans

I dreamed of walking across maps much of the night.
   ~Gary Paul Nabhan, *Songbirds, Truffles, and Wolves*

   . . . And something evermore about to be.
~William Wordsworth, *The Prelude, or Growth of a Poet's Mind*

Preface

I was seven years old, alone and wandering the ancient streets of the *shuk* in the Old City of Jerusalem. All around swirled the myriad language of merchants, tourists, beggars; the alternately pleasing and offensive odors of spices, incense, cooking, urine, sweat; the visual array of thousands of items for sale, from carved camels to hookahs to mysterious confections.

I was not lost. My family had moved from California to Israel for six months while my father took a sabbatical. He researched history at Hebrew University and we connected with distant family, the offspring of my great-grandmother's sister Sarah who had emigrated from Kyiv to Palestine before Israel declared independence. Her family had fled religious persecution when their homeland was about to begin the turbulent and rapid transition from the Russian Empire to the Ukrainian People's Republic to the Soviet Union. Sarah was still alive and we enjoyed meals with her and the rest of our newly met kin. This direct connection to pogroms and exile suddenly made me a participant in the progression of history, and not merely a happy-go-lucky bystander. Though it took some time for this to sink into my consciousness, the fact of our living in Israel created a foundation upon which I would learn to view the threads of the ever-unfolding human tapestry.

I knew much of Jerusalem by heart at this period when it was safe for a child to roam freely without supervision. Perhaps because I was so young, it did not seem bizarre to stroll into the church where Christ is said to be buried, or to touch the massive rock upon which Abraham intended to sacrifice Isaac. So began my lifelong love of adventure to foreign lands. So began the sauntering—another way of saying that walking became a sort of religion to me, whether in a new city, through a forest, or just along the familiar streets of my neighborhood. At a more basic level, I always feel better after a saunter, no matter how poorly I felt before.

* * *

Until recently I would tell my poetry students to see the world. By this I meant not only to be aware of what was around them, to *engage*, to stay awake—I still encourage them to live like this. I also urged them to go out and experience other countries, not just as tourists but as travelers who are motivated to learn customs and languages. When you immerse yourself in different cultures, it grows increasingly difficult to place people in boxes, to see any ethnicity as *other*. This comes from heartfelt interaction with people you would never have imagined spending time with. Besides the fact that travel broadens your literal and metaphorical horizons, I believe that if most everyone got the chance to explore the globe, wars would be diminished due to a commensurate magnification of compassion and patience. And those from economically privileged countries would learn to live in more generous and humble ways.

Why would I stop suggesting to students that they go abroad? Air travel is the easiest and most popular method to do so. But of all the forms of transit, it vies with road transport as the primary contributor to climate change, and I no longer condone it. Though I might risk alienating some readers, it bears saying that I consider recreational flight a fatalistic indulgence and have my doubts about anyone getting on planes at all. In the face of current and impending environmental upheavals, our species' continuing behavior relating not to just airplanes but to consumption itself—to what we choose—exhibits a quintessential, psychic disconnect from our responsibility for what is happening, and from what needs to be done. Perhaps soon this will have seemed an extreme stance, but perhaps it may have turned into the norm. At the time of writing this preface, it has been four years since I made the decision not to fly until a significantly cleaner mode is established, possibly using hydrogen power.

So this book is a contradiction in that it celebrates international travel at a juncture when humans need to stay put. I began writing the poem before the crisis of climate change had entered common consciousness, before our predicted dire "weather events" had become reality. I wanted to share how walking has informed my life and served as a means of discovery, in both far-flung places and in my own neighborhoods. And I wanted to show how the simple act is a metaphor for moving forward in life, regardless of one's obstacles or doubts. I was not bothered that many books on the subject were already written, both in poetry and prose. Rather, I took this as a challenge to render my own unique perspective in as compelling a way as possible.

* * *

Near the beginning of Part Two, when my father died, I address the fact that not everyone has the ability to walk. I posit that they *must grasp the wings of birds, / Imagining what I cannot: / Their minds as wings, their thought / As song...* It may be only a feeble, even a failed, attempt at reckoning with what I cannot imagine. But it is an attempt at acknowledging all people, all readers or listeners, hoping that in the reading of the poem, they are borne to another place for the moment—ultimately, the "Holy Land" of existing in the present—which is what I feel in the very best moments.

As the poem unfolded, it grew evident that I could most successfully convey my message by revealing a lifetime of such instances, and so it developed into an autobiography. Just a handful of specific people are featured. It must suffice that they represent not only themselves, but also hundreds, maybe thousands of others who inspired me and drove me onward.

One of them is John Nelson who lured me to Peru and Bolivia and took on the role of sometimes wild, kaleidoscopic guide. Another is my lifelong friend since the first grade, the artist Daniel Davidson. We had known each other for eight years when my father died in 1980. I was fourteen then. Death forged a further bond, as Daniel's father—a banker in San Francisco—had been murdered in 1968 by a schizophrenic youth who sought revenge for being denied money. He claimed that the Beatles had a secret bank account with millions of dollars for him and he was trying to make a withdrawal. Our early losses unexpectedly brought Daniel and me closer together, especially as teenagers when we were establishing our identities, seeking profound truths and meaning in the universe.

Joining me in Southeast Asia were my spiritual brother, forester Paul Harper; and our forever iconoclastic companion Matt Yadley who ended his odyssey in 2021 and whose spirit I hope now saunters in peace. Matt and Paul and I were shown around the ruins of Ta Prohm at Angkor in Cambodia by a fifteen-year-old named Eart, pronounced somewhere between *Ee-el* and *Yurt*. Her family lived just outside the temple grounds and did not have enough money to allow her to begin attending high school. Our connection was so deep that when I returned home I got in touch with a nongovernmental organization to see if I could participate in funding her education. Though someone I spoke with on the phone eventually met Eart, she did not qualify for aid from the NGO and my quest sadly faded away. However, this experience helped me to see how peregrinations can transform into pilgrimages.

* * *

My partner Jennifer Rand has walked with me perhaps more than anyone else and always makes our shared path seraphic. She often hiked with me and our "niece," Tulip the basset hound, who also makes an appearance here and has since journeyed on. Jen offered invaluable advice as I revised the poem. As usual, my literary family from the Lost Coast Writers Retreat also assisted with this project, specifically Vinnie Peloso. Additionally, Jim Dodge lent his raptor-keen powers of discernment to the editing process, unintentionally confirming my belief that I needed to compose in ballad stanzas: quatrains of lines alternating four and three beats. I was compelled to write in such a fixed form to capture my years of walking in a kind of song.

A giant redwood of thanks goes to the same team who created my first book. My cherished friend and collaborator CM Phillips of SequoiaSong Publications was the artistic and exacting designer. Kyle Morgan at the Press at Cal Poly Humboldt (formerly Humboldt State University Press) provided the requisite enthusiasm and professional support. This book is a co-publication of both presses, with SequoiaSong publishing the print version. Stacy Becker valiantly consulted me about detail and intention as she drew the illustrations, striving to convey my vision while staying true to her own muse. May they all—as may all my readers—saunter sunward.

Jev L. Levinson

December 2023
Azalea Hill
McKinleyville, California   xiii

I

Once more I step into the gloom,
Abandon lands I know,
The shadows reaching for my bones,
The candle dusking low.

Those unknown voices call my name
In language beyond fathom,
In accents strange and guttural,
As steeped in laudanum,

Hypnotic as the waves on shore,
Relentless as a pulse:
Resistance fades as I stride forth
Despite my gut's convulse.

By languages and dreams I'm drawn,
The hint of something more—
By mountains terraced to their peaks,
By whispered ancient lore

Of spirits dwelling deep in trees,
Of oracles in caves
Who see our paths mapped in the stars,
Who foretell early graves;

By flavors born of spices rare,
Melodic chants and those
Upon my ear cacophony
Like raging beasts' death throes

Until, that is, by firelight I've
Sat and supped and danced
All night until another dawn
Made tintinnabulant

Whatever sound I'm graced to hear.
No longer dissonance,
This music of once-far terrain
Dispels my arrogance,

Dissolves chains that thwart my senses.
Oh let me sense anew
This world with all its protean ways,
Devise the passe-partout

To open heart and mind and soul
To wonders vast, minute.
The secret is a pilgrimage,
A track that will transmute

Quintessence gray and visionless
To ether almost pure,
A trade wind gusting through my veins,
While footing grows more sure.

It is to walk that we are here,
A taking of the day
(Or those who blossom eventide—
In darkness they assail

The doubts that plague the seething brain
And learn a light within),
It is advancement of the blood,
A touch of Bedouin,

When purpose is a thing fulfilled,
To be: divinity.
Divinity I questioned long.
I sought a single key

To access answers, to connect
A feeling—intuition
Of a higher power—*energy*—
With some set tradition,

Some scripture and attendant mode
To which I could be true.
And so I sampled sundry creeds,
Religions I pursued,

Partaking of their cryptic rites,
This impulse toward meaning,
Enraptured by the lotus petals
With Buddha's eyes serene.

Yet Buddha cut the threads of context,
Emptied of the endless
Quest: beyond my comprehension,
Beyond all no and yes.

The triangles of David's Star
I traced as though a charm,
Tefillin with their hidden scrolls
I wore on head and arm,

Inherited symbology
Bound in my family's core.
The Eucharist, the bread and wine,
I swallowed, restored

Awhile, and understood the cross,
But gravitated to
The Mystics' esoteric form,
The magic rendezvous

Of opposites, dualities
That join, *mysterium
Coniunctionis*—alchemy—
The meeting to illume

This animation that we are.
In search of ritual,
In application of doctrines,
All felt conjectural

Though I savored the spark of each,
Forever would cherish
The peace of each, recall solace
When I felt impoverished,

Hold them in my heart as touchstones.
I always heard the trees
And songs of birds and ocean's roar,
Such tones that could appease

A restless psyche, and always
Felt attuned to wind, rock,
Earth itself, abiding devotion
Released me from the clock.

To see the world as religion,
Then, to know the planet
As a passage toward the self
Which is a rivulet

Before its return to cosmic dust:
Ceaseless topography.
It all began in the holy land,
Brought with my family,

Immersion in another life
For half a fateful year.
Just seven, then, as I became
A global traveler,

Awareness scant of history,
Or purpose, variance
In belief or identity:
I drifted as by chance.

Though happy in naïveté,
Half-happy when a world
Awaits awash in colors, depths,
My very being was curled

As a fern frond tight in shadow
Till photosynthesized
With sun, releasing oxygen,
Rich soil vitalized

Roots, white-tipped, seeking sustenance.
Suburbia encased
My youth, homogeneity
A blanket that erased

The grit imbuing genesis
Of passion to transform
Knowledge to imagination.
Scarce guides there were to warn

Against this shroud, complacency.
In books and songs they spoke,
Awakening my nascent muse
And casting back the cloak.

My fortune that I was so young
With preconceptions few,
Absorbing difference thirstily,
Assimilating Hebrew

In alleyway and marketplace,
The schoolyard throughout spring—
Bet Sefer Haim Arlosoroff—
Apricot pits bargaining,

A game that all the students played.
Deprived of Arabic
By a certain insulation,
A separation thick

As a medieval citadel—
My family over *here*,
Among Twelve Tribes of Israel,
Religious atmosphere

Unspoken spurning of Arabs,
Though tolerating *them*:
As if aberrant lineage
Malformed from the same stem,

Vocabulary parallel . . .
I would yet rub shoulders
With those who heeded Allah's name,
Knelt daily five-fold prayers,

My language matrix nonetheless
Electrified by tongues
From every corner of the globe—
And after all, these spun

From Aramaic long ago,
Before the great divide.
Left free to roam Jerusalem,
Explore the countryside,

Alone or with my brother Dave
(Since Aaron was just three)
I ventured to the Western Wall
Within the old city

And chatted with the shopkeepers
In their long djellabas,
Some long-bearded, some missing teeth,
Their hookah stimulus

For another day at their stalls,
Their trade inherited
Through generations of forebears.
Tobacco scents and bread

Fresh-baked mingled with the spices:
Cloves, cumin, cardamom
Infused my senses uninformed;
Mint, paprika, saffron

With urine blended, a mélange
Tinged with blood of carcass
Hook-hung—sudden tang of sheared copper
In my nostrils, this mass

Of marbled meat begrimed with flies,
This bulk of . . . sheep? or pig?
A donkey-cart clattered down stones,
Narrow passageway thick

With gathered hagglers all now forced
To press against the wares,
No heed to this boy horrified
Pushed to the thing midair—

13

Slick sinew, muscle, gristle, fat,
But nameless in the fear—
Who stopped his lungs as he was kissed
With a sickening smear,

While seconds seemed to stretch a year . . .
The world redefined.
And the cart rolled onward. It left
A pristine world behind,

The boy now wedded to this land,
A kiss bestowed by death,
The counterpart to all he knew,
The spirit through a breath.

Armenian, Jewish, Christian,
Muslim, navigation
Through the four quarters, harmony
Among these religions

Within ancient cobbled city,
Millennial buildings,
Caves carved from the strata of time,
Dome of the Rock's gilding,

Such shrines of sacrifice and birth,
Ornate censers swung by
Berobed men, orthodox, they seemed
Eternal, a reply

To those who walk a separate path
That Christ would never leave
Them lorn. Yet this accretion of worship,
Muezzins' cries that weave

Another tapestry, hands with
Eyes on their palms, turquoise
Paint upon a village's doors,
So many losses, joys,

All bound in systems of belief,
And focused in one-third
A square mile within walls
Outside of which goatherds

Meander, seeking hillsides green
Below the Olive Mount,
Three-thousand-year cemetery,
My family in this ground—

Accumulation of ethos
Instilled inner searching
For an answer to these questions,
This life deciphering.

We traveled through the desert lands,
Connected with our kin
Transplanted when our ancestors
Splintered from their origins,

The czars of Russia bludgeoning
Their sacred hearths, acquired
Through degradation, brutal force,
Murder, took what they desired.

A music, then, that ventured back
To realms in picture books
Informed the fabric of my days,
Condemning those who took

Away the only life evolved
From struggles biblical.
(Did they not traverse the Red Sea,
Flee in furtive trickle

To live nomadic forty years;
Fly the Inquisition;
Migration to foreign borders
When the institution

Forbade they worship as they wished,
Depart beloved homes
Perhaps to settle where the Reich
Would someday mill their bones?)

Exulting also with the wind,
Or singing like a spring,
Remembering that praise is due
On wakened summer wings.

I heard it from the instruments
Whose tones took on the cries
And bleats of livestock, hummed like bees,
Creaked like salt that dries

Along the Dead Sea's arid shores,
Evoked dry bones—Levite
Ezekiel in prophecy
Watched flesh on Canaanites

Return, with tendons, hot red breath—
That all returns, once more,
To source. And so I changed, devoured
By centuries of lore,

And opened out to what might come,
Never thinking soon would
Be the wrecking of my father,
A man who understood

That I might someday stray afar,
Reject religion if
Inspired by another music,
Enticed by arcane glyph

Encountered in my hegira
From loss toward meaning.
The intersection of the crash—
When I had reached fourteen—

Returned to California,
One mile from our home,
His classes over for the day,
Topography well known . . .

Where an epileptic driver
Caught in sudden seizure
Smashed her car into my father's—
The next four months a blur—

Would be the end of my dreaming
As brought down by a curse.
In coma with his broken bones,
Suspension—nothing stirs—

His glasses and his wristwatch lost:
I could hardly see him,
The man, the friend, abiding force,
Metal pins through his limbs,

His spleen would have to be replaced,
He breathed with punctured lung.
An operation on his brain.
No more words from his tongue,

No more history, dear professor,
No more songs, sweet cantor.
But in this time I did not think
My final view was here,

This hospital: no thought so far.
Not ours to know how long
We have with souls wound 'round our hearts,
How long until they're gone.

II

Before the months of coma—his
Imposed, mine reaction—
Already I was challenging
Authority, traction

Gained, or so I thought, in willful
Negation of the norm.
To question all the words of law
And never to conform;

Comply with dour expectations
Seemed closing all the doors,
Especially when hemmed by streets:
Monotony deplored.

The orchards razed for houses new
While forests sang to me—
But these I could not reach, too far—
Out there lay mystery.

Accessible within two years,
The mountains and the coast;
Adventures launched with big gray car
Toward what beckoned most.

My hair grew long, my feet grew tough,
Forged leather, free of shoes.
Why separate my skin from earth?
Was I not free to choose?

A decade yet to read Chatwin,
Though four years before Thoreau,
My guides who galvanized my thoughts
On what by birth we know.

These bare feet carried me for miles
Through woods, on beach, boulders
Climbed as with Dan Davidson I
Fit skin to stone contours.

The best companion I would know,
From naïve six until
Adulthood, the rare creative
Impetus, miracle,

A mirror to what I believed,
That pen and ink could bring
Both truth and truth of fantasy.
I heard the sirens scream

Again; it was the first of June
When Mother said *He's gone*—
The day before released my dad
From coma stretching on

For years for all she guessed. She told
Him he could cease the fight,
The spirit free from flesh, leave off
Hovering in twilight.

Somehow she knew if he awoke,
A fragment of the man
Would linger, languish, just a ghost,
No more historian,

No more a leader of the tribe,
Perhaps no more to speak
Or laugh or recognize her face.
She knew she had to seek

Another way of being alive,
Despite this final grief.
Her words and tears sank to their **mark,**
And he became the breeze.

A dream I had three decades hence:
He journeyed on a boat
And turned his face to catch the wind,
A gentle breath afloat,

In absolute tranquility,
A message telling all
Was well. Even then, as I dreamt,
His cherished brother Al

Began descending, father figure
Tarrying only days
On earth—the news to reach me yet—
And I would never gaze

Upon his form again. The dream
A gift, a blessing from
My father, a reassurance:
The zephyr we become.

Had Father lived, but could not walk,
How then to go forward?
It falls to those without the means
To grasp the wings of birds,

Imagining what I cannot:
Their minds as wings, their thought
As song, the beating heart itself
A covenant begot

By powers beyond reckoning.
A taking of the day
For all, going à la Sainte Terre,
The Holy Land, the way

Ahead for all who live: *There goes*,
Thoreau declares to us,
*A Saint-Terrer, a Saunterer,
A Holy-Lander.* Yes,

Significance for what we are,
Significance of step—
Uncover grails for our own tongues
By cross or minaret.

To saunter, long ago, it is said:
In reverie, to muse;
A definition fitting well
For those who roam for clues.

For some, the language yokes the land,
A practice to progress
From desolation to the sun;
A resurrection. Yes,

Imagination it must be,
Or muscle to the wheel,
To render meaning from a void,
To want once more to feel.

The day my father left this world,
I wandered on the streets
Unthinking, found myself before
A door. A bittersweet

Reunion this would be, when Dan—
Not seen in many moons—
Accepted such a vagabond.
I sensed we could commune,

Recalling that he had also
Had his father taken
At an early age, not yet three,
As violently, a sin,

The cleaving murderous knife through his back
In false retribution—
More violent, then, for the intent . . .
Dan knew destitution.

Reality had lost a sheen.
My mind was unprepared
For total absence. Innocent
My trust my dad be spared

From death. His coma not entire,
But a threshold between
Consciousness and darkness. Could he
Hear us? See us? It seemed

He could, but not respond, blue eyes
Rolling slowly side to side.
No one had warned me. A scepter
Slipped and shattered as he died.

Marie asked how my father fared—
She knew my pain, had lost
Her man, three children now to raise
Alone—but I was washed

By an endless surge, bereft of words
Or even thought, how could
I voice incomprehensible
Betrayal? . . . No. The flood

Would choke my throat and vomit would
Erupt, profane the air.
Okay, I lied. *About the same.*
But soon she was aware

That I moved in a haze, from shock:
My mother called their house,
For I had disappeared, no note—
She sought my whereabouts.

Without my knowledge, Marie disclosed
My secret to my friend.
He held it close, did not divulge,
And guessed that I wound mend

In time as he had done. Dan knew
Why I could not speak the words,
Bestowed the haven of friendship
That to this day endures.

Two years would pass before we found
Ourselves rejoined, high school
A bridge that spanned our neighborhoods,
Awakening the lull

In our rapport, brotherhood beyond
The blood of home, this new
Alliance steeped in exploration
Of music, art—we grew

Into a deeper love of all
This life can be, a search
That never ends for what provides
The sanctity of church.

From children we'd transform to men,
Embrace both freedom and
Responsibility for earth;
So in these days expand

To beings who could steer their fates.
We spoke of everything,
Imbibing joy, confronting loss . . .
On a summer evening

At last my true friend confided
He had shared my burden
That day my feet had guided me
To his street, let me pretend

My father still remained among
We quick. A twinge of shame
For my deception shuddered through
My heart—yet felt no blame

From him, no judgment, for there was
None. I felt his sympathy
As another heartstring with mine
Pulsed the same melody.

The feet more sensible than mind—
I learned to trust their traipse:
As thoughts be thick and turbulent,
The spirit navigates.

With Father buried in the ground,
Now Mother forged a plan:
Return to Eretz Yisrael,
Elude quotidian

Routines, old ways where we'd be numb.
My brother Dave had lost
His bearings, drifting here and there,
A mental holocaust

Enshrouding when our patriarch
Succumbed to the summons
Of eternal sleep. Oblivion.
Catastrophe that stuns

A being so supersensitive
That, as children, at word
Upon our cousin's sudden death,
Dave's eyes at first were blurred

And then went blind for half the day.
He anesthetized his mind,
Withdrew. With miscreants in darkness
His life became aligned,

Forsaking love of family.
Alone he spun. Abroad
We left, then, shy one sibling, six
Weeks with the roots of God

And taking time for other lands,
Castellan England, France,
The pyramids of Egypt, on
The Sphinx's countenance

I gazed, approached the monument—
The guard agreed to take
My hat with Union Jack as bribe.
The African sun baked

My bones, but still I loped around
The Sphinx, every angle
To hold in memory, our bus
Pulling from the tangle

Of tourists and dust, Mother
Pleading with the driver
To tarry for her stray. With death
Reality, I swore

That while I paced upon this earth
I'd savor moments such
As these. Would I return someday?
Even so, could I touch

The Sphinx again? In my seething
Youth, I found that *moments*
Mattered most, those spots of time as
Wordsworth tells, more intense,

More crystalline—yet molten too—
Than minutes ticking by.
To walk is the benediction,
In step we vivify

The soul encaged in sinew, held
Here in the vale asleep,
Cocooned throughout our days, ensconced
The way we keep our feet

Swaddled, unsullied, yet betrothed
To sun and wind and mote
Of all touching, as incarnate
We wear this human coat.

So toughened were my feet, ingrained
With dirt of commerce, tombs,
From untold thousands of years, each
Night the residuum

I washed away in ritual,
A holy cleansing, apt
Here in the holy land, and all
Beyond. So I had mapped

Jerusalem those years ago,
Could navigate all roads
And lanes by rote, wandered, long-haired,
Exactly as I chose.

The gashing of one foot by glass,
Perhaps a mile from home,
I hid from family, stanched the blood,
Wore shoes awhile to roam.

Beginning to glean the costs of war,
Embattled land I trod,
Collected souvenirs—bullets—
Saw peasants hunger-gnawed;

Strolled buildings blasted, split by bombs;
Awoken in the night:
Katyusha rockets found their mark,
The villagers in flight.

Awakening to imbalance,
Alert to affluence
And poverty, my mind had lost
Its springtide innocence—

So fate decreed: engage the vision,
If only crudely formed:
A consonant existence, all
The people to be born

And die, and all the species, yes,
Enkindled by the sun
(Or by whatever agency
Vitality's begun),

To be and to be understood,
To dwell without trespass,
Invoking native tongue, behold
The other, looking glass

An aperture upon the strange.
Convey recognition,
Reciprocating royalty,
Inherent unison,

A reciprocity for being.
I deemed it would be words
With which I'd reach the hearts of those
Whose souls, as seeking birds,

Desired self-revelation,
No mere anthem to chant.
A validation of their voice:
To be significant.

We reach each other a thousand
Ways, through pictures, music,
Architecture of the spirit,
Cuisine that makes us lick

The marrow from our psyches' bones,
The memories that hoist
Our heavy brains through mud to sun:
These sparks that summon choice.

Ten thousand workshops I would helm
Someday—unbeknownst
To me in youth—uncounted poems
Wrought from the innermost

Core of young and old. They would listen
To these hallowed texts (some
Composed within the year, yet who
Would know? typed, they become

As metal plaques affixed to stone).
In calling forth the muse
My students would delve into regions
Of pure light—or abuse—

Portray their hopes and tragedies
In written rhythmic lines,
Reciting newly minted songs
As vital as their spines.

III

Throughout my vernal years, at home
And Israel again,
To ramble became obsession,
A sort of discipline:

Immerse the self in the nascent day,
Discover different tracks;
Whatever weather wraps the sky
Dictates the moments' syntax.

Indiscipline was intermixed,
Hauled from the void I'd seen,
Accelerated recklessness.
Alone in a ravine

With darkness closing in, I clambered
Up sheer rock face, skin torn
By stone and bramble, compulsion
To ascend, damn the thorns,

And slipping once as gravel spilled,
Suspended by one hand,
Silence waiting below, the swift
Imperative, command

To endure propelled my free hand
To seek an implausible
Crevice. A finger's friction held,
Suspended on that wall,

The slightest shift of weight and one
Toe grazed a subtle notch,
Enough security to rest
And press. My first hand caught

The knurl above, then on I climbed,
Emerging from the gorge
To live another day, to trace
My own arteries, forge

An odyssey of risks and dreams.
The climb was one of many
Times I barely missed an early
Grave, an audacity

That sparked my blood: I blazed as though
Immortal, dared my fate
And laughed to find myself alive.
I intoxicated

Myself with exploits scintillant,
If vacant to the costs.
Careening down a mountainside
Too steep, one ski was lost,

My body hurtling, the second
Ski's tail jammed fast in snow,
A sudden wrenching of the knee,
An injury I would know

Until that day I know no more.
(When I had lived nearly
Half a century, this transformed
Into my Inca knee,

Reawakened to pain as I
Scaled Peruvian ruins,
Kept pace with six-foot Dutch Marlous;
Bolivian full moon

Bathed Isla del Sol, and Johno,
Rambler of continents,
Dimensions, revealed high temples,
Realms beyond immanence,

Escorted me to Qalla Q'asa,
The Pisac citadel,
Across houses of the holy,
Great terracing upswells—

Self-urged to explore while I could,
This wound a sacrifice
To primal Apu mountain gods:
This pilgrim's flesh their price.)

Thus exposed to such a world,
I yearned to wend it all,
Unearth the beauty of this earth,
A quest devotional

And everlasting, adventure
That both sates and creates
The curious nature, places
One places that embrace—

At best—the outlander; sometimes
Spit one out, alien
Entity momentarily
Condoned, a ganglion

Intrusion in an otherwise
Autarchic, insular
Organism, such circumstance
Shattering the glamour

Of global connectivity.
Sometimes the tribe demands
Invisibility, a need
To shun the caravans

That pass with shifting destinies—
A being endemic
To its particularities
Isolate, systemic.

To test myself against their ways,
To see how I might fit,
To speak a different language,
Experience transmit.

In understanding foreign thought,
Surrendering my creed,
I hoped to hear the beating hearts
And words of deities,

And all the while pace new terrain,
To taste the desert dust,
Be painted with volcanic ash,
Fulfill this wanderlust.

Descend to caves where swarms of bats
Swirl into nightly hunt;
Or trudge through mud of mangrove swamp,
Regard the warthog's grunt;

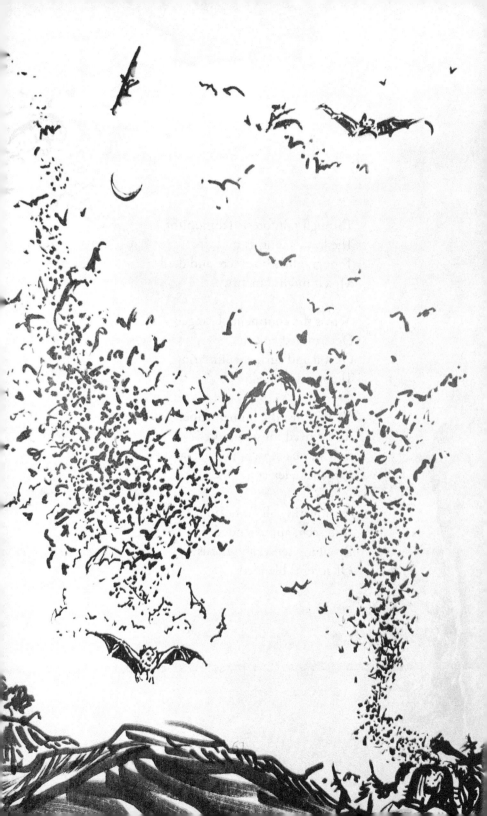

Through rainforests I'd monitor
The lizards long as I;
Topographies both sere and dank
Myself might sanctify.

Across the continents I ranged,
Determined citizen
Of soil and surf, encountering
The many-folk akin

To all of us, the human tribe.
All I'd need for weeks on
End was backpack, journal, and pen,
Concoct a lexicon

Assimilating all I'd heard
And seen, apprehended
By all my senses, synthesis
Of accents blended

From nations often small enough
To seem quaint curios.
A Moroccan conversation
New friends and I composed

In Essaouira, seaside town,
In English, Arabic,
French and Spanish, dash of Berber,
Lingua franca plethoric

As tongue met tongue searching insight.
Gibraltar caves, macaques
That chat about a stolen meal;
Long beaks of storks that clack

Like windup motors shutting down;
Surreal architects
Adorning Spain with Borgesian
Design forged to vortex

Prosaic passage, rearrange
The daily patterns, meant
To shock the very soul—unveiled
Spirit be immanent

In mortar itself, not merely
In shapes of cherished things:
To climb the spirals of Gaudí,
Depart on womb-wet wings.

Electric glacial frozen blue
Past alpine Grindelwald
Imbued this pneuma with legends,
Primeval creatures cold

That prey upon unwary, rash
Excursionists, enfold
Them deep in clear cruel cloaks of ice,
Trophies for their strongholds.

Evermore would glaciers haunt me,
That incandescent blue:
New Zealand, Norway, Alaska—
Cavernous Xanadu,

A dreamtime threat, became as though
Incarnate malady;
To crave the taste of honeydew,
Forbidden ecstasy,

A wish for warmth amidst the ice
Forever closing in
As age entombs the spark of joy
Known only by ripe skin.

Cerulean, a state of mind,
We chase it all our lives:
The Rockies, Andes, ascend the heights.
Impermanence connives

Despite a golden thrice-weaved charm.
Still, castles call the seer
To trace our labyrinthine yore,
Sing as a sonneteer

Of glory gone and yet to come,
To praise the cobblestones,
Achievements of the bygone clans
Who fashioned jeweled thrones;

To sing the hillsides and the heath,
Be schooled by murmuring streams,
Or whispers of the druid trees,
The sun's subsiding gleams.

To England, France, and Germany,
Vintage Europe I must rove,
Their counterparts with other codes
To comprehend I strove:

So Scotland, Ireland, Italy
Meandered, Austria . . .
Unexpected disembarkings
To find empyreal

Desmene, lonely lanes, ancient groves . . .
Some nights without a bed
When plans unraveled, ill-prepared,
Scant sleep on jacket spread

On grass by lakes where I would bathe
In early light, stoic
To the chill, then find my road, some course
Toward some hearth, stout stick

In hand I'd tramp in hope of meal
Or wheels that would take me
To the village, commerce, culture,
Partake of bonhomie.

This utter anonymity
A tabula rasa
To those who gazed, engaged, bemused,
Conjured utopia—

Sweet times before a filtering web,
Devices that distract,
Information diminishing
The act, the now: *infract*—

Just you and me, some food, a book,
Laughing at translation;
Imbibing piquant anecdotes;
Creeds in syncopation.

A consecration of the other
Through eyes that finally see;
Adopt the beating heart once shied
Until the strange is me.

Whole cities I explored on foot.
A room in pensión,
A good night's sleep (or so one prays)
And I was in the zone,

Awake to simple nourishment,
Then amble avenues,
Esplanades, back streets, arteries,
Content if I should lose

Direction, for I had nowhere
I need be (excepting
Sites signal or renowned, if time
Constrain), the day machine

For what need be, return to map
Unfolded, guidance sought
From passersby, reap the beauty:
Segovia wall, wrought

Medieval, enduring, backdrop
For the everyday folk—
Kaleidoscope for me and symbol,
A hundred walls evoke—

So textured over centuries
With brick, then wood, then stone
At distinct heights, interlayered
As kings overthrown

Resulted in neglect, chaos . . .
Yet denizens remained,
Applied the earth with craftsmanship,
Age- and element-stained,

An artistry, a gallery
Of life itself, colors
Unimagined by devotees
Of chroma, so enspheres

Me and as I recall this wall,
It is as if this life
Is one of multitudes, impulse
Of eternity rife

With borders formed only to be
Slipped, disintegrated.
Asylum Scandinavia
Disclosed my aggregated

Lives, spun visions without warning
Of who I used to be.
I stood behind my right shoulder,
On a vessel at sea,

Observed myself transcribing logs
In quondam language—
My apparel antiquated—
Not of my heritage.

Another day a graveyard passed
Sprung locks within my mind:
I witnessed—*felt*—generations
Of spirits unconfined,

Humanity in ceaseless sequence:
At tasks; in love; by rote;
By seed to soil to sun to shadow:
Ephemeral zygotes,

We all-absorbing status quo
Hunger for perfection,
Yet seldom tread perfection's path,
As though we live again.

An energy like molten wax
These northern lands exuded,
A magic glimmered palpable.
Across years exalted

I dwelt among a Swedish clan,
Three women isolate.
A summer home, once family farm,
Swiftly activated

This sense the land was sentient.
Outside of Harnösand,
Remote—the reedy lake our bath—
Beneath a pine I'd stand

As time dissolved, untold minutes,
Convinced *something, some being,*
Abided just beyond my ken
And if my hearkening

Were pure and absolute, a veil
Of perception would tear,
An entity emerge amid
The trees. I must beware.

As ardent my desire to behold
A creature worthy myth,
A fear consorted with my will:
What powers would permit

Such trespass into territories
Unsanctioned? What revenge?
I scarce breathed, blending with the woods . . .
Faint sound and I would blench . . .

Repeatedly I'd halt my tracks,
Discerning unknown things
That never did reveal themselves.
Creatures inhabiting

The lands were sworn to have been seen—
This mountain with the face
Of a witch *is* a witch asleep;
This boulder does encase

A wizened troll; the countryside
Comprised of numinous
Otherings. I could only nod
Assent as I looked, *yes*.

Some echoes as chimerical
Resounded 'round the globe
As on I went, as I immersed
In thermal pools, disrobed

With crazed Mustafa underground,
Beneath Hierapolis,
Caverns hidden below Roman
Retreat, an interstice,

A secret of the plebeians—
Today's Pamukkale,
Cotton Castle of calcium,
A city sightseers stay,

The minerals cascading down
A mountainside, a white
Swath against a brown hinterland.
Trance-perceived stalactites,

Dreamworld formations, lost dwellings
Of Cappadocia,
Hittite refuge from Thracians
As Anatolia—

This religious, statecraft crossroads—
Endured incessant onslaught.
So churches subterranean
Were made where eyes cannot

Detect: and in Meteora
Were placed impossibly
On pinnacles, insulated:
Belief's tenacity.

Ah, caves, ancestral memories,
Candles by the Mekong,
Access only by the river—
To strike the temple's gong,

A summons of the Wat Pho bats,
Rich incense, Angkor Wat,
Arouse the sleeping gods; Ta Prohm,
The strangler figs cast knots

Throughout the jungled edifice.
Young Eart would be my guide,
Meek and lovely, wise, unhappy
Heir of Khmer genocide,

And yet she offered me her heart,
Allowed a glimpse within
The mysteries of fathomless
Affinity, my kin,

Somehow, my teacher that our souls
Are all conjoined and blind
To anything that does not give
Sustenance to ours, bind

Us each to each. Further nations
This wayfarer has known,
And further still someday to go,
In company and lone.

Companions—scores—have shared my stride
Through deserts, garden glades.
At times we spoke as citizens,
At times as renegades.

In heat that turned our foreheads blue,
Keffiyat bleeding dye,
Or rain that caused our feet to mold,
Or cold that made us cry

We knew we walked a righteous path,
Intent to augment love
Among all beings within this vale.
To tread the deepest grooves,

To enter one another's sight,
Explore a moment's truth,
To give ourselves to sheer motion,
Our contact our pursuit.

The exploration in itself
A giving to the day:
Discovery of what persists
And what is swept away.

IV

I have traversed my neighborhoods
As though a faithful gear
Commanded by a universal
Force. Humankind coheres,

Elaborate mechanism
Of deed, desire, strength, verve,
Of introspection, industry—
(Myself, and those I serve

With words, connecting hemispheres,
Laughing at looks askance
From those who find me too expressive—
That *snap* intolerance—

For often I have taught their young
In schools, instilling wonder
Of the strange, of what is Other:
Ignorance to sunder.

So many offspring reached, the tide
To turn to openness
That someday all will walk as free,
Horizons limitless)—

Communities as canvases
Being painted by our being,
In cities thick with enterprise
And rural steads pristine.

Once home from Europe, first solo
Roam, my feet compelled me—
Circadian—become the lanes,
Prowl upon filigree

Forest pathways, feel the streets
Of Santa Cruz, ocean
Nest of nature, Bohemia
Of my soul in motion

And rendered Picasso sculpture
On beaches, in cafés,
Become the map, become the day
Or Vesper star ablaze.

So blaze this life by one's abode,
Not only when afar.
Forsaking academia,
Pursuit irregular,

I briefly toiled alongside Dave,
My lifer stagehand brother,
Constructing sets and running lights
In amphitheaters

Throughout the San Francisco Bay.
Disoriented now,
I pressed against Oakland concrete,
Forced myself to plow

Those urban blocks where I subsisted
In rented room, often
Rambling more idyllic Berkeley—
The place where I began

My journey—leafy neighborhoods,
Venerable dwellings,
And shops that spoke from an old groove,
Locus of happenings,

A time of revolution gone
Yet held within our hearts.
Another year in Santa Cruz,
Then northward to new parts:

Arcata, Humboldt, dubbed the Shire
By children of the flower.
Deep behind the redwood curtain,
Burgeoning ambassador

To planet earth, learning the ways
Of coded rhetorics,
Political, academic,
Inheriting beatniks'

Ideologies, composing
Poems tinged with voices
That rippled from the Native tribes,
Terrestrial noises,

Uncompromising defenders
Of pure and sacred lands—
Ebullient upon trails and roads,
I met custodians

Who chained themselves to ancient trees,
Ecosystem guardians
Devising weirs to save the fish
Instead of requiems

When all would be too late. This seemed
A place I could not leave,
A sanctuary of like minds
Along the ocean's heave,

Where I could stride entire lives
Yet never memorize
The wending mountain slopes: this scene
Ordained to internalize.

But chasing knowledge by degrees
In universities
Led me to a third immersion
Far from my beloved trees.

Across the country, Greensboro
In North Carolina,
Industrial metropolis,
Inverse utopia

To where I had torn my roots from soil
So nutritive to what
I felt could generate a forest,
Forever grow uncut.

The promise, though, of poetry—
This quest I must engage
Amidst intense humidity;
Prolific foliage

Of climate new, electric air;
Unaccustomed culture;
These, with obsessive scholars, forged
A new literature

That stitched the texture of my brain
As if the textile mills
Were weaving my idealism
With the blood in the hills:

Annihilated Saura Tribe;
Colonists and Redcoats,
Where I sunned in Battleground Park;
Plantation slaves; mere motes

Now disregarded by most who
Tread the pavement. And yet
I savored ice cream at a counter
History cannot forget,

That Woolworth five-and-dime become
Museum since, testament
To change. In a world of porches,
Autumn benevolent,

Declining sticky summer heat,
Sweet afternoon iced tea,
The cicada atmosphere seeped
Into dreams, and altered me.

What woodlands I could find transmuted
A spirit sometimes lost
On civic surfaces, for I
Maintained my rambles, crossed

Chaotic boulevards until
Pines and vines enveloped
Perception, primeval terra
Firma, sultry sky cupped

My core and corpus. Companions
Joined on many days, they
Recalled childhood jaunts, and trusted
My motions to assay

The Blue Ridge Mountains, dependent
Solely on hoisted gear
We carried on our backs, their first
Rustic, sylvan ventures

They would continue when I left
Historic College Hill,
Those streets routinely promenaded
With banter, verse, goodwill.

I could not stay when the work was done—
Pursue the search for more.
Another university
I sought: deeper explore

Romanticism's influence
Upon the galaxies
Orbiting in Wallace Stevens'
Cerebral majesty . . .

But this was not meant to be, this
Ensconcing, position
In the tower, on committees:
True academician

I was not, am not—too much
An artist. Returning
To Humboldt, unsure of my path
Among the evergreens,

I thought to teach collegiate prose—
One last degree I earned
But quickly grew dissatisfied:
For poetry I yearned.

Throughout the years my little songs
I've written as I've walked,
Composing more while teaching youth:
To thousands I have talked,

Imparting love of craft, and lore.
And so, it seems, my days:
Dictations of observances,
The sifting of a phrase.

The pen to page akin to tread,
A certain freedom found
Within the lines, as Wordsworth's sonnet,
That scanty plot of ground.

Yet freeing the mind as foot meets earth,
Release of roiling blood,
Expansion as the cells inspire
The heart's breath-giving flood—

This motion moment free of wish,
In motion is my being.
In ranging by the six rivers
(And those beyond decreeing

By some appointed agency,
For nearly twice that number
Flow along these vales), I have known
A sense unencumbered

By boundary of any kind,
A final curtain lifted
From my vision, as though the neurons
Of my brain were shifted

By a force beyond reckoning,
A moment absolute
As all else falls away. There is
Nothing else, no pursuit,

No need to fill. These woods, these slopes
And steeps, and meadows, all
Integrated with what I am,
Sauntering the ritual

That both loosens and binds, creature
Pure of pure creation.
Another creature, innocent,
Adjusts my gait to a run,

As by my side a basset hound
Rejoices when I free
Her from the yard, exuberant
Tulip, her energy

Conjoined with mine and the bouquet
Of the forest, this black
And white and brown bestower
Of cheer on woodland track

To all who, beguiled, meet us
Along our way, pausing
For indulgence. Overzealous,
Overheated, between

Two aerial trees Tulip will lie,
Reluctant to resume
Our excursion, comfortable
Now in the verdant bloom.

Eventually we recommence
And I am satisfied,
For it is as simple as this:
The day is sanctified

By having hoofed from in to out,
And a sanguine sweetness
Imbues the afternoon—a kiss
From my ambassadress.

V

Had I the means, I'd walk the world
Entire, propitiate
The songlines, sing solidity
Unto earth, ambulate

Away the days, not *killing* time
But questing beyond clocks,
A mining of the inmost self,
A certain orthodox

Approach. To walk into religion,
Unwritten in some book,
Would be itself the discipline,
A course for me to shuck

All roiling thought and simply saunter:
All loam the holy land.
To walk into meditation,
The trail as talisman,

Peregrination as prayer—
We forget each breath is
Prayer and so create our shrines,
Remain in chrysalis,

Our wings obscured by wit and sheen
When all around the air,
The sun, the green, the senses beckon
Our arctic marrow, prepare

Our transport into essence true,
Becoming whole of now
Until the body is the god:
Through blood we make this vow.

The feet unfold the pace of mind.
At last, vision is free.
Unloose the layers self-imposed:
Crystal lucidity.

These feet create a path anew:
Filament invisible
To follow, thread to tapestry
Mirrors terrestrial

Trajectory, echoes canals
Along the Inca streets,
Ollantaytambo labyrinth
Or where Lake House repeats

The archetype . . . By night the feet
Can feel the routes unseen,
These eyes of the darkened forest
Sidestep plodding routine,

Descry layers concealed by doctrine,
They know a naked truth,
As when the living face appears—
Its aspect absolute—

At dusk, autumnal equinox,
Embedded in a tree
Where limbs fork into trunk and hold
The shadowed space, augury

Of change and always deathlessness.
His ageless gaze regards
Me as it would a leaf before
It falls, yet says with bards

That I have found my lineage,
By song and sojourn graced.
Eternal calm emanating,
A comfort so enlaced

Within my being that my heart
Can for the moment bear
To cease beating altogether,
No more need to prepare

For departure, the still point found.
Upon a cushion seated;
In lotus—still—returning home;
Squirming thought quieted:

Endless breath of meditation,
Uncoiling what we know.
Such stillness, ripples left behind:
A mind of indigo.

So walking is the holy breath,
As much as the retreat
And burgeoning unto petals
In hush serene, complete—

The walking is the breath of all,
A being of the day,
No matter if in orphic woods
Or down an unsung byway.

The streets outside one's door suffice,
Even in a scabrous town,
For all momentum culminates
In sovereign peace profound:

Intention ever be the key,
The will to be elsewhere—
Enough, for now, if rooted firm,
Or easy in the chair,

So long as you are with these words,
You are one who saunters.
We travelers of this terrain
Greet the spirit, and endure.

Someday these feet shall walk no more,
Yet I shall be content;
The day complete in all its stride,
Without impediment

When language sloughs off all its fears.
Emerging from the cave
We cast about ourselves—the darkness
Ransacks; seeks to engrave

The slab of who we are—we squint
In stupefaction, what
Course to take where meaning stays, how
Navigate clear of ruts . . .

It is this simple: odyssey
The condition of growth,
Every walk indeed a mission,
Adherence to an oath

As proffered by Thoreau. To walk
The pace of every day,
Perhaps a tranquil roundabout,
Or map for Saturday

When travel is the mode of life
And weekends stretch to months . . .
To walk into divinity,
To heed the chants of monks

Or worship hymns sung by the wind . . .
To walk into the holy:
Your door opens on a temple:
Approach this mystery.

Without a walk the day is not
Fulfilled: substratal sense
Of bliss suffuses body, mind—
Zoetic opulence

Pervades the self until the self
Evanesces, flesh be
Fabric woven with wind and rocks
And sticks, stitched tapestry

Ever-changing. The spell thorough
As cares fall to the dust:
Old absolute, dogged definite
At last diaphanous.

Once more I step beyond the gloom—
At hand, oblivion—
Behold the way so seldom seen
And walk into the sun.

About the Author

Zev Levinson is the author of *Song of Six Rivers* and editor of *The Jews in the California Gold Rush*, written by his father Robert Levinson. He brings poetry into classrooms and other sites through California Poets in the Schools.

To learn more about the author, book a poetry reading in your community, or set up a poetry workshop in your school, visit his website at www.zevlev.com.

About the Illustrator

Stacy Becker has worked in education and nonprofit arenas for over 35 years around California's Wigi (Humboldt Bay), Central Valley and East Bay areas. She is an occasional illustrator and constant admirer of the North Coast cultural and environmental scene.

Made in the USA
Monee, IL
20 October 2024

68037012R00075